# The Official
# Guide to
# Dysfunctional
# Parenting

# The Official Guide to Dysfunctional Parenting

Frederick Muench, Ph.D., and Gregory Nemec
Illustrations by Gregory Nemec

**Andrews McMeel
Publishing, LLC**

Kansas City

08 09 10 11 12 RR2 10 9 8 7 6 5 4 3 2 1

ISBN-13: 978-0-7407-7247-4

ISBN-10: 0-7407-7247-3

Library of Congress Control Number: 2007934135

www.andrewsmcmeel.com

For Jodi, Sammy, and Lionel. I love you. —F.M.

For Kat, my partner in dysfunction. —G.N.

# Foreword

By B. Terry Brazelton*

Dysfunctional parenting comes as naturally as learning to crawl. So, you may ask, why write a how-to book about something we have already mastered with no real formal training? Aren't the influences of television, society, and our own imperfect upbringing enough? While all of the above are useful, they tend to contribute to the process subconsciously. Wouldn't you like to be completely aware of your innate dysfunctional child-rearing abilities? Haven't you wondered about all of the areas of dysfunctional parenting that you may have overlooked? By following these simple suggestions, you can rest easy with the knowledge that you know exactly why your children are in therapy.

---

* No relation to T. Berry Brazelton, noted pediatrician and author.

  B. Terry Brazelton is not a physician and is, in fact, fictitious.

Cry over spilt milk.

When the new baby arrives, tell the older children that their turn is up and it's the baby's turn to be loved.

———————

Don't drive with your infant on your lap unless you're on quiet country roads.

Tell them bad dreams are God's way of telling them, "Be good or this will happen for real."

———

"Don't let the bedbugs bite. Really, be careful."

When they say, "Mommy, I'm afraid of the dark,"
reply, "Yeah, I see what you mean. All kinds
of dangerous things are probably just waiting
for you to turn off the light."

———————

"Remember to breathe tonight while
you are sleeping."

"Did you put on your tracking device?"

_____

Guide your child into friendships with fellow
preschoolers with vacation homes.

Three-year-olds understand rational arguments.

**Q:** Why am I here?

**A:** Because we had no idea it would
be this much work.

**A:** Because I needed someone
to love me.

**A:** We had to shut up Grandma and
Grandpa somehow.

**A:** Because I went to the liquor store
instead of the pharmacy.

Inconsistency is key.

———————

Take him to the emergency room
each time he gets a mosquito bite.

Potty-train her on a really big toilet bowl.

Be sure not to put your kids in your will,
or they will kill you.

———

Routines make people boring.

"Bob, Bob, Lionel only hit four out of five
developmental milestones this month!"

When he goes to the bathroom, scream frantically
that part of his body is falling off.

———————

Run to your baby every time he makes a sound
or he will hate you forever.

"Honey, be careful near the electric cord."

"Have you kids seen my bong?"

Everybody is out to get your children—
everybody.

———

Instead of using their names,
start referring to your kids as
"the overly sensitive one,"
"the disobedient one," or
"the one who needs help in math."

When money's tight . . . ask them to choose which one of them will get sent to the orphanage.

―――――――――

Before they leave the house,
tell them to comb their hair
so people don't think you're an alcoholic.

If your toddler tends to use her left hand,
sew her left sleeve to her shirt
so she switches to the "correct" hand.

**Q:** Are we there yet?

**A:** Of course we are.
This highway is just a crazy hallucination
you're having during a seizure on
Grandma's living room floor.

**A:** If you want us to leave you
on the side of the road, then yes.

**A:** If by "there" you mean the boulevard of
broken dreams, then, oh yeah,
we are definitely there.

Kids make excellent shoplifters and beggars.

_____

Chicks will dig a man more if he's
at the zoo with his "niece."

Rated "R" means no one under seventeen, *unless* accompanied by an adult.

**Q:** Why am I here?

**A:** I had no friends and mommy
groups are a great "in."

**A:** Three months off work sounded
good until the three months were up.

**A:** To save our marriage . . .
and you know how that worked out.

If your neighbor calls your kids "healthy,"
assume she thinks they're fat.

———————

Describe all the possible reasons why they
shouldn't talk to strangers.
Be very graphic.

———————

Make them color in the lines.

Have a life preserver handy at all times.

Say yes, then no . . .

then yes . . .

then no again . . .

then, a little later, yes . . .

then no again.

Promise them, "After the game we'll get ice cream
. . . if you win."

———————

Make them go to the bathroom
at exactly the same time every day.

———————

Teach them about other cultures:
Have them become Jewish on Christmas,
a Jehovah's Witness on their birthday,
and diabetic on Halloween.

Deep-breathing exercises get you through those
horrible two weeks between the end of camp
and the beginning of school.

———

Gifts make up for not being there.

———

Just because they're innately drawn to something,
it doesn't mean your life plan for them is wrong.

Constantly remind your kids that
outside the house is a very dangerous place.

**Q:** Mommy, why does that man have only one leg?

**A:** He did something really bad.

**A:** He kept picking at a scab
    on his knee.

**A:** He's probably Canadian.

**A:** A man with one leg? Run!

If you read to your children,
they'll never learn to
read for themselves.

———————

The coach just can't see your child's natural talent.

The best toy is the most expensive one.

If the preschool teacher, the kindergarten teacher, the first-grade teacher, the principal, and the school psychologist all identify the same problem with your child, change schools.

———————

What the books don't tell you about healthy sleep habits in children: *There is absolutely nothing you can do.*

**Prada** = self-confidence

**Spelling errors** = a time-out

**Wheatgrass juice and cauliflower** = snack for Little League

**Foreigners** = hilarious or dangerous, depending

*Hustler* **magazine** = the "birds and the bees" talk

**Wetting pants in public =**
teachable moment

**Birthdays =** quiet time

**Ritalin =** cure-all

**Happy Meal =** happiness

**Botox =** happiness forever

Coach your kid's Little League team
and ignore him or her.

Coach your kid's Little League team
and ignore the other players.

**Q:** Why is the sky blue?

**A:** What's wrong with blue?

**A:** Actually, it's not blue.
The atmosphere is made up of
colorless gases. Water vapor refracts
the white light from the sun into the
spectrum . . . well, you're just not
smart enough to understand.

**A:** Nobody knows! The universe is a
scary mystery we shouldn't even
try to comprehend.

**A:** Be glad it's not another color,
because that could mean a
tornado is coming.

Teach them that when they find themselves
in unpleasant situations, they are most likely
powerless to change things.

————————

"Mommy, I want—"

"Okay."

Mark their height an inch lower each year,
and tell them they are shrinking.

If you don't scream "Oh my God!" every time they fall, they will think you don't care about them.

———————

Tell little Ruttiger his older brother is named after you because you love him more.

Kids learn what not to do by watching your mistakes.

When they bring home artwork,
use it as a coaster.

Prolonged absences make you seem
intriguing and edgy.

———————

Kids don't understand anything you say before
they are five years old.

## When the School Evaluation Says . . . *It Really Means*

Spirited . . . *Annoying*

Careful . . . *Wimp*

Thoughtful . . . *Crybaby*

Energetic . . . *In need of medication*

Confident . . . *Obnoxious*

## When the School Evaluation Says . . . *It Really Means*

Gifted . . . *Social outcast*

Content . . . *Boring*

Assertive . . . *Asshole*

Social . . . *Slutty*

Charming . . . *The next Charles Manson*

"Do you want to play baseball, Dad?"

"We have all the baseball we need
right here on the TV."

———

Give your five-year-old son a two-hour haircut.

———

Play *Let's Make a Deal* for their birthday.

Nervously suggest they shouldn't go down
to the basement after dark and don't explain why.

Remind them to look happy
in front of your friends.

———————

If your child asks if he can smoke like you do,
tell him he's still too young.

When your son gets glasses,
tell him they make him look "less stupid."

If they ask why you are taking their picture,
tell them that things don't sell well on
eBay without one.

———————

Mix together several jigsaw puzzles with similar
color schemes and watch the magic happen.

"Ready for church?"

**Q:** Where do you go when you die?

**A:** Into the cold, cold ground.
Or if you prefer, the crematorium.

**A:** I forget . . .

**A:** Depends. If a car hits you, you go
to hit-by-a-car heaven.

**A:** Don't worry, Mommy and Daddy
will never die.

"Mommy, last night I dreamed
I was a ballerina superhero
and a pony rider in the circus!"

"I used to dream."

———————

Playing Scrabble with a four-year-old
will surely boost your fragile ego.

Attend parent-teacher night in a blue bunny suit.

Take an interest in their visits with your ex:
"How was your visit with Mommy and her new
friend? What did they say about me? Don't lie,
I know she said something. Well, it's not true.
Who are you going to believe, me or her?
He's not as good at baseball as me."

———

"Mommy, look at that butterfly!"

"Get in the car."

When they ask for a puppy,
tell them that if they hold that stuffed animal long enough
it will turn into a real puppy.

Hide their Easter baskets under the floorboards.

Holding your kids back a few grades will give
them an edge in competitive sports.

---

Frequently put off their punishments. This growing
"discipline debt" should keep them in line.

If they refuse to go to bed, warn them,
"If you don't go to sleep right now, you might die."

———————

Assure your daughter that she really
will be pretty one day.

Allow them to invite only rich kids to their birthday parties.

Pick one night a month
when the family can eat together.

———————

It's all about you.

———————

Make empty threats.

"If you lean over too much,
your eyeballs may fall out of your head."

**Q:** Why am I here?

**A:** Because I trusted Daddy.

**A:** All those celebrities look so cute pregnant.

**A:** I was hoping to create a perfect little replica of myself.

Drive the family to an amusement park.
At the front gate, express disbelief at the
outrageous prices and drive home.

———

To calm fears about getting their tonsils out,
tell them, "Tonsils don't do anything anyway.
Let's just hope you don't need them
to get into heaven."

Redo their artwork.

———

"You're going to break your mother's heart. . . .
No, no, it's fine. . . . Change the channel. . . . I just
hope she handles it as well as me."

You know that crunch you hear when you bite into
a potato chip? Tell them that's the sound
of it crying.

————————

Push them into childhood entertainment.
They'll spend a lot of time away on location and
will need someone to manage their money.

**Live your dreams through them.**

"Only wake me if someone is bleeding—and not a tiny scrape bleeding, either."

———————

Help them learn self-discipline by eating all their Halloween candy in front of them.

Stay your kid's favorite: Make sure the nanny is always the one who says "no."

———————

When they complain, "That's not fair!" tell them, "Of course not. Life's not fair. That's why you have to cheat."

Be brutally honest when they make you gifts.

If they say they want to go to the water park,
tell them, "Me, too, but your father doesn't,
so don't blame me."

———————

Appear on a reality or daytime talk show
with them.

Constantly express your worries about life.

**Q:** Why did Mommy leave?

**A:** Well . . . your room was
pretty messy.

**A:** She did?

**A:** From now on, Tiffany will be
your mommy.

"I'm nervous about going to Jacob's house
for a sleepover, Dad."

"I would be, too!
Their house has that weird smell."

———————

When you take them shopping, pick out their
favorite foods, look at them for about five seconds,
and put them back.

**Project:** Hire an actor to walk silently around the house in tattered clothing. Ignore him completely. Refuse to believe your children's claims that a strange man is in the hallway.

Teach them to say "Thank you" only for things they really want.

———

If they tell you they got a 98 on their nuclear physics exam, ask them what happened to the other two points.

If you don't know the answer to a question, make something up.
The longer they think you know everything, the better.

If they ask why you have so many more pictures of Sammy, explain, "Well, he is the firstborn, and it's so much more exciting the first time around."

———————

"Mommy, I'm tired."

"Imagine how I must feel."

Punish your male child if he plays with dolls.

A child can't cry or complain
if his mouth is full of doughnuts.

―――――――

"Daddy, can we go to the father-son picnic
this Saturday?"

"Oh, silly, you know I play golf every Saturday."

When leaving them with the babysitter, say,
"Hopefully we'll be back later. If not, don't worry.
Jodi's responsible—that's why we hired her."

"I love you, Daddy."

"I'll give you fifty dollars if you shut up."

—————

If you do their homework,
you don't have to take the time to explain it.

Remind them that Mommy will always be there
to fix every problem. Now come here and hug Mommy.

Never negotiate with your children—
just belittle them until they give in.

—————

Avoid using profanity when telling your son
his kindergarten teacher is hot.

If they complain during a long car trip,
threaten to pick up the next hitchhiker you see
so that they'll have something to complain about.

**Things to totally freak out over:**

• Field trips

• The fact that one of his feet seems to be slightly larger than the other

• The guy at the grocery store who looked at your kid with "that look"

• Petting zoos

## Things that will probably work themselves out:

• Otto's interest in matches, Lysol, and the cat

• Odd little hand-rolled cigarettes you find in your son's pockets when doing laundry

• Your high school daughter's thirty-year-old boyfriend

• The bingeing, the purging

**Q:** Looks like Amelia needs braces.

**A:** There goes the trip to Disney.

**A:** Oooh . . . I hear that really hurts.

**A:** I guess your school picture this
year will be a wash.

**A:** But her older brother's
teeth are perfect!

When your daughter is seven, tease her about her "boyfriends" constantly. When she hits puberty, pretend boys don't exist.

———————

"Daddy, I'm scared."

"Wimp."

Make them wear clothes you liked at that age.

**Q:** Why am I here?

**A:** Because I couldn't find meaning in
my life any other way.

**A:** Tax write-off?

**A:** Because condoms are only
99 percent effective.

**A:** We assumed the third time
would be a girl.

Periodically ask,
"You're going to medical school . . . right?"

———————

"Don't forget your lines,
or people will think I am a moron."

"If you're going to play like a girl,
then you should dress like a girl."

**Q:** Why is Uncle Jimmy always with his friend Steve?

**A:** Uhhh . . . how about some
ice cream?

**A:** Because Steve is a lot thinner
than Uncle Jimmy's ex-wife;
remember that, Sarah.

**A:** Just don't touch him . . . or he
could turn you into the gay, too.

**A:** Look, the important thing is this:
I'm straight and you will be, too.

## THE BEST TIME TO STOP THE MOVIE RIGHT BEFORE BED

---

***Snow White, E.T., Peter Pan, The Iron Giant:***
In each of these films, turn off the TV right after
a major character "dies" but before they are
magically brought back to life.

***The Wizard of Oz:*** Dorothy is imprisoned and
awaiting execution, the hourglass is running out,
and the wicked witch appears in the crystal ball,
mocking Dorothy's cries for Auntie Em.

***It's a Wonderful Life:*** George Bailey brings his children to tears with his cruelty, then leaves to commit suicide.

***Willy Wonka and the Chocolate Factory:*** Charlie and Grandpa Joe, terrified, are inexorably lifted toward the giant whirring ceiling fan.

***Taxi Driver:*** Never stop this movie.

The more choices you make for them
the more you will get your way.

———————

If they complain,
"You love Margaret more than me," reply,
"You had to find out sometime."

"Why ya always reading?"

**Project:** Find some photos of you and your children when they were very young and digitally insert an older, unfamiliar child. Print out your retouched photos, frame them, and display them around the house. Then, when your children misbehave, tell them, "Your older brother Horst used to do that," while pointing to one of the pictures, and leave it at that.

Whenever you have a meeting with your child's
teacher, bring your attorney.

_____

If your son doesn't want to go hunting,
don't let him eat any meat.

"Just don't bleed on the new carpet."

**Q:** Is that Santa, or one of his helpers?

**A:** Nope.

Remind them to only beat up kids
whose fathers are smaller than you.

———————

If your children notice a dead animal
on the side of the road, ask them
if they have seen the cat recently.

———————

Your daughter doesn't like to wear dresses?
Pray the gay away.

"First place gets to go to college."

# CHECKLIST FOR GIRLS

**Age 1:** Relax! You can coast for another year. She's just a baby!

**Age 2:** Start her on the fat-free diet.

**Age 3:** No more PBS. It's for babies.

**Age 4:** Continue to monitor her weight daily.

**Age 6:** Reveal to her the sacred prophecies about the imminent Armageddon.

**Age 8:** Get her subscriptions to all the celebrity gossip magazines.

**Age 10:** Ask her when she is getting married.

**Age 12:** Ignore her requests for information about her changing body.

**Age 13:** Give her short shorts with "JUICY" printed on the backside.

**Age 14:** Relax! Parenting really stops around this age.

# CHECKLIST FOR BOYS

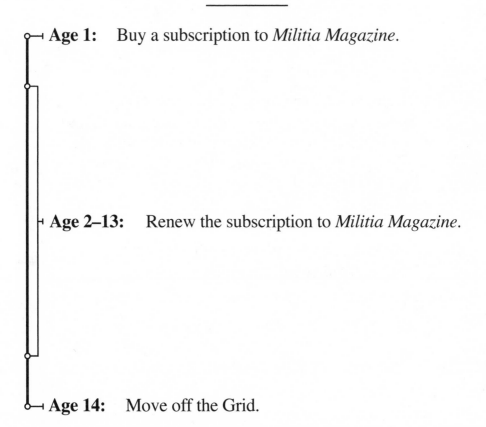

**Age 1:**   Buy a subscription to *Militia Magazine*.

**Age 2–13:**   Renew the subscription to *Militia Magazine*.

**Age 14:**   Move off the Grid.

Remember, even though you drink every night, spout racist comments, and cheat on your spouse, it's the trash they're learning in school that's warping them.

———————

When you unwrap that Father's Day tie, say, "And you expect me to wear this?"

"When I said 'some quality time,' I meant for me."

**Q:** Why am I here?

**A:** Mommy and I wanted to feel all grown up.

**A:** Have you ever heard of grain alcohol?

**A:** We screwed up pretty bad on your older sister, so you're like a do-over.

Watching *Mommie Dearest* together will make them reassess your parenting abilities.

———

When shooting baskets with them, praise them with, "Good shot, but it was probably luck."

A nice sixteen-ounce single malt scotch will relax you
when talking to them about the dangers of drug use.

If your daughter studies hard and
gets an A+ on her test, say "A perfect score?
Wow, it must have been an easy test!"

—————

Favor the better-looking kid.

Remember . . . it's *your* science project.

There is no way to control your child.
Once you come to this realization,
it's easy to let them do as they please.

———

When moving to a new place,
your child may express concerns about
making new friends. Suggest that if they don't,
there's always the Internet.

When asked about sex, laugh.

"You're punished for a week, mister!"

"But there's a great party tonight!"

"Uh, starting tomorrow."

**Project:** When puberty hits, children are extremely self-conscious. Take a recent picture of them and have it retouched so it looks about forty years old. Then show little Suzy the remarkable resemblance she has to a childhood photo of her aunt, the bearded lady.

"But why weren't you invited to that party?
We need to make you more popular . . .
maybe get a pool or something."

———————

If you aren't getting through to your teenager,
yell louder.

Occasionally ask, "So, Stevie, do any of your friends think I'm a MILF?"

———

Constantly remind them of all the mistakes they've made so they don't make them again.

———

Spending as much time away from them as possible fosters healthy independence.

**Mention that as they grow older
they will look more and more like you.**

"You can't tell me what to do!"

"You're right, son. I am sorry."

———————

"You know you should treat me better, Inga.
I will die someday . . . maybe soon."

Volunteer to chaperone every school dance.

**Q:** Mom, I have a pimple.

**Well honey, pimples are just nature's way of saying . . .**

**A:** Scrub harder.

**A:** Your diet and hygiene are dreadful.

**A:** You're meant to be alone.

If your son says, "Mom, I want to try out for the hockey team," tell him, "Bobby, that's your brother's thing, don't you think?"

———————

Hand them pimple cream
before they leave for the prom.

Going away to college will give them too much independence,
will loosen your grasp on them, and will leave you too
much time for introspection. Buy them a car, a boat—anything.
But don't let them go.

Teach them to always do what their conscience tells them to do—unless the popular kids are doing the opposite.

———

Remind them that Nostradamus said the world may end very, very soon.

———

"Of course spelling counts! Don't even try if you can't spell everything right!"

**Q:** Where do you go when you die?

**A:** To heaven, if you always do exactly as I say.

**A:** By the time you die, you'll probably be converted into food for the starving millions.

**A:** I guess to the same place everyone who belongs to our religion goes.

**A:** I don't know, but you can't bring your toys.

# Afterword

So you've done all you can do and your children have been sent out into the world. Don't relax—your job isn't over. Your distance from their lives should only enhance your desire to control them. Don't forget those 3 a.m. phone calls to make sure they are safe, to ask who that is with them, and to remind them that nobody wants to marry somebody who's easy. Or frigid. Or too focused on work, or underemployed, or overweight, or skinny. And when they beat all the odds by actually marrying and reproducing, your grandchildren provide the perfect opportunity to test out all the old tricks. Don't hold back, because this time you won't be the one who has to clean up the mess. But also remember this: When you are much older, and need to be fed and bathed and driven places, your adult children can always refer back to this book for advice on dealing with your "second childhood."

# About the Authors

Photo: Katharine Nemec

Frederick Muench, Ph.D., is a clinical psychologist and the director of clinical research and development at a stress-management company. He has held faculty and adjunct faculty appointments at Columbia University College of Physicians and Surgeons and New York University. He lives in Brooklyn, New York, with his wife, Jodi, and their two *perfect* sons, Sammy and Lionel.

Gregory Nemec is a freelance illustrator whose work has appeared in books, magazines, newspapers, and educational material. He teaches a weekly preschool class for three-year-olds, and he teaches older children all kinds of art, from drawing to animation. He lives in Pleasantville, New York, with his wife, Katharine, their children, Jacob and Olivia, and a somewhat ignored cat.